FOREWOR

This footpath guide is complementary to Walkabout Series which describe walks in Leea walks described in this publication have been chosen to enable walkers to enjoy walks in some of the Parks and in the older suburbs of Leeds, and to read a little of the history of these areas.

   As with the other books in the Walkabout Series, the intention of this book is not to describe the quickest way of getting from place to place, but to follow an interesting route, and see how the older buildings have been woven into the fabric of our modern communities.

   The walks also pass through some of the wonderful Parks of Leeds, enabling the walker to enjoy the benefits of the formal gardens and landscaped areas so close to the City Centre and all the associated traffic.

   At the time of writing it is believed that all the footpaths used in these walks were designated as public rights of way or as permissive footpaths. It should be borne in mind that diversion orders may be made from time to time. Similarly arrangements for parking cars and bus routes are altered, and it may be advisable to check routes and times.

CONTENTS

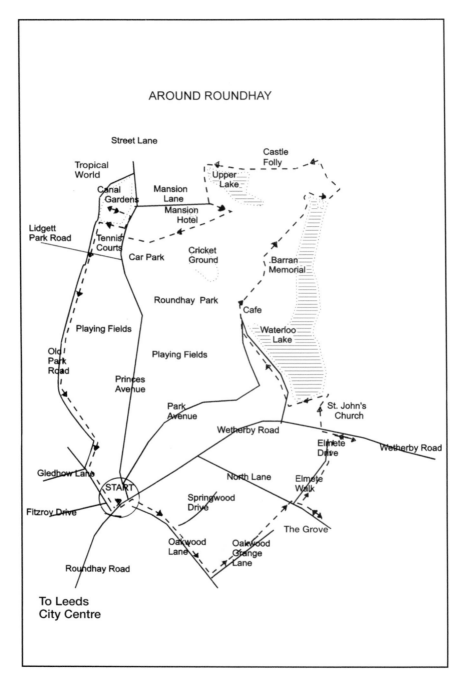

AROUND ROUNDHAY

Street Lane

Tropical World

Castle Folly

Upper Lake

Canal Gardens

Mansion Lane

Mansion Hotel

Lidgett Park Road

Tennis Courts

Car Park

Cricket Ground

Barran Memorial

Roundhay Park

Cafe

Playing Fields

Waterloo Lake

Old Park Road

Playing Fields

Princes Avenue

Park Avenue

St. John's Church

Wetherby Road

Elmete Drive

Wetherby Road

Gledhow Lane

START

North Lane

Elmete Walk

Fitzroy Drive

Springwood Drive

Oakwood Lane

Oakwood Grange Lane

The Grove

Roundhay Road

To Leeds City Centre

AROUND ROUNDHAY

Start: Oakwood Clock.   Map: OS sheet SE 23/33
Transport: Frequent buses. Nos 10,12,19,21,44.
Car Parking: Free at Oakwood Clock.
Description: Easy walk for all the family. Town scape and park paths.
Approximately   6 km. 4 miles   2 hours.

This walk starts at Oakwood Clock which stands near the car park and bus stop.

> *The clock was originally in the covered market in Leeds, Vicar Lane. It*
> *has been a landmark at Oakwood since 1912. There is a plaque on the*
> *wall of William Brown, Estate Agent across the road commemorating*
> *the clock.*

Cross the road by the traffic lights carefully towards the Post Office.

Oakwood people are lucky to have a post office, and a useful number of shops including a rather unusual fish and chip shop. The front of the fish and chip shop is chrome, glass and green laminate and it is a listed building. The Estate Agent, William Brown was formerly the local post office (transferred to the present site in 1962) and more recently a branch of LLoyds Bank. See the plaque on the front of the building.

Cross Oakwood Lane going towards the public library building on the opposite corner and turn right up Oakwood Lane.

Oakwood Lane was once known as Horse Shoe Lane. Probably a reference to the fact that there once was a smithy near by. The Public Library building was built as a private residence which had stabling at the rear with room for a carriage to draw up and let the owners of the house alight in the safety of their own drive.

As you go up Oakwood Lane you will see many large houses both in brick and stone. Near the top of the hill on the right hand side is one of the largest built in stone. It is now a nursing home called Sabourn Court, (once Oakwood House).

This house, much altered now, was built in the 1820s for Robert Hudson in a classical style. It gives you an idea of the size and grand manner of dwellings that were imagined for this area when the Nicholson and Elam estates were being developed.

Continue on Oakwood Lane. Almost opposite Sabourn Court there is a very attractive building called Tudor Lodge for very obvious reasons.

Notice the large stone pillars on either side of the entrance. These have elaborately carved wreaths on them. This lodge was once the lodge entrance to a large house called Towerhurst which belonged to the Penrose Green family, commemorated in the Churchyard at St Johns. The house no longer stands, its grounds have been taken over by a housing estate.

Continue up Oakwood Lane and you will soon see another building that was once the lodge house for Springwood House.

Springwood House, now known as Frazer House, stands behind the lodge. This house was once lived in by one of the many members of the Lupton family. Frazer House belongs to Leeds City Council.

Continue on Oakwood Lane passing some newer houses to reach Oakwood Grange Lane. Turn left along this road. Pass Oakwood Walk and Tatham Way on your left. On the right you will enjoy seeing some excellent 1930s type housing. You will also see Newton Lodge on the right and Newton Court. Behind here used to be the original Newton Lodge

Through a gateway you can get a glimpse of a large house, Oakwood Hall. Once known as The Acacias, it is a handsome house with extensive grounds. It was once the home of Darnton Lupton.

Continue on the left hand side of Oakwood Grange Lane. The footpath narrows as you approach Oakwood Court and is bordered by a wooden fence on the left and a wall on the right. At the T junction with Oakwood Green a short diversion to the right brings you to an imposing house called Eller Close.

Eller Close is well maintained and it is now several flats. It was built for William Ledgard a woollen manufacturer who had mills on Wellington Street.

After having looked at Eller Close return along Oakwood Green and turn right on to Foxglove Avenue. The new St. Johns primary school is to your left. Turn right again on to North Lane for approximately 150metres.

As you walk along notice the wall on your left. It has some very large stones forming supportive triangles, and has a castellated top.

A little further on the right hand side of the road is North Grove and on the left is The Grove.

Once the home of James Milner who was President of the Civic Trust. He was a hero in the 1914-1918 war and awarded the MC and bar. He was Deputy speaker of the House of Commons, M.P. for S.E. Leeds, and a partner in the firm of J.H. Milner, Solicitors.

Both these houses stand in their own grounds. The Grove has much larger grounds than North Grove and is a listed building. They were built for the Burton family (woolstaplers in Leeds)

After having seen the Grove houses return to North Lane and retrace your steps for approximately 200 metres till you come to a post box on the corner of Elmete Walk, turn right down hill, and turn left on Elmete Drive to reach Wetherby Road. Cross Wetherby road with great care, turn right with the Roundhay Park to your left. Very soon you will see St. Johns Church on your left. Go through the gates and up the slight hill towards the Church.

St. Johns Church was designed by Thomas Taylor and built in 1824-1826 by Stephen Nicholson, one of the family who owned Roundhay Park before it was purchased by the then Mayor of Leeds, John Barran in 1871. It is interesting to spend some time looking at the Church and the memorials to some of the well known citizens of Leeds.

The striking memorial to the Penrose Green family, of a large marble angel with a broken column, stands in a prominent site at the side of the path. There are also monuments to the Luptons, Baron Airedale of Gledhow and Joseph Whitley who was father-in-law to Louis le Prince one of the pioneers of motion picture photography with his film taken of traffic on Leeds Bridge in 1888.

St John's Graveyard

6

After enjoying some of the splendours of St. Johns go back to Wetherby Road. Turn left to look at the alms houses and the old school building, also built by the Nicholsons for the benefit of their retainers. Turn round and walk back past the Church gates to the car park below the Waterloo Lake dam.

This car park was the site of a very popular open air swimming pool until the early 60s. The steep embankment used to feature a waterfall coming from the lake. Keep to the right of the car park and go up hill through the wood till you reach the large lake. Turn left and cross over the embankment with the lake on your right. Turn right at the end of the embankment and go along the main carriageway. You are now along side Waterloo Lake, said to be so named because it was completed in 1815 in celebration of the recent victory over the French in the Napoleonic wars. The lake is very popular with fishermen and it is seldom that you will pass this stretch of water without seeing some hopeful fisherman. Continue along this flat tarmac road till you reach the cafe, a popular refreshment place with splendid views over the lake. Leaving the cafe go through the car park and take the right hand road going up hill now closed to traffic.

Back in the sixties there was an aviary and a small maze near here, also the original wooden cafe building.

Continue up hill till you come to the stone domed drinking fountain erected in memory of John Barran.

This memorial was a feature erected by John Barran himself to try and solve the problem of drinking water in the park for people who needed refreshment, (before the days of the cafe). The fountain was erected in 1882 to designs by Thomas Ambler (who also designed the Moorish-Gothic building in Park Square). John Barran was a wealthy industrialist who was instrumental in Leeds Council buying Roundhay Park when it came on the market following the death of one of the Nicholson family. The area to the left of the carriageway is used extensively for concerts and sporting events.

From the memorial go diagonally down across the grassy slope to the north end of Waterloo Lake. Go right round the head of the lake, turn left, and after twenty metres turn left over the old stone bridge and follow the track passing the Castle Folly to the upper lake.

The Mansion

> *Both lakes are said to have been created from old quarry workings. Waterloo Lake is deep and sometimes in summer there are boats for hire available. The upper lake is much more shallow and has many ducks, swans, coots and moorhens that enjoy the attention given them by many generations of children and adults who feed them. Sometimes one can see a heron there.*

Walk along by the head of the lake, to the right is a miniature railway which operates during the summer and at holiday periods. Turn left over a stone bridge over a small stream coming in to join the lake and turn up hill to reach The Mansion. It is said that there was once a mock hermits hut along side the lake on the left. If it was there it has long since disappeared. At the top of the hill is another small car park and in front is The Mansion.

> *The Mansion House was built by Thomas Nicholson, designed by John Clark, and completed in 1826. It has been used as a restaurant since 1873, and by the Gilpin family since 1884. William Henry Gilpin was a horse breeder and furniture dealer of North Street originally. It was said that he desired the tenancy of the Mansion so that he had more room for his horses. The Mansion was developed as a restaurant and has become a popular venue for dances, weddings and celebrations.*

Go clockwise round the Mansion and follow the narrower footpath past the garden for the elderly and disabled, pass the garden dedicated to the blind, and reach the exit to Princes Avenue.

Princes Avenue is so called because Prince Arthur the third son of Queen Victoria came to Leeds to declare the new road and the park open to the public in September 1872.

Go down left to the pedestrian crossing, cross and turn right passing the toilet block and go up to the entrance to the Canal Gardens. Enter the gardens and take the path with the canal on your left, go right through the arch in to the Rose Garden. You will then see a large conservatory and the cafe to the right.

The Coronation House (as it used to be called) was built in 1911 and has been rebuilt and extended several times in more recent years due to the generosity of Mr. Arnold Ziff. It has become one of Britains top tourist attractions with the aquarium, butterfly house etc. There is now a small charge for admission. This area with canal and enclosed garden was used by the Nicholsons for growing fruit and vegetables. A small separate garden contains the Garden of Harmony and the Globetrotters Garden developed by the students of Askham Bryan College in partnership with the City of Leeds. The whole area is now known as Tropical World.

A pleasant hour or two can be spent in the Tropical World and the cafe nearby. Across Princes Avenue in what was the old stable block there has been another development to make a welcoming hostelry if you fancy a more substantial meal. The Roundhay Fox is a very popular venue with young and old.

Near the entrance to the park there is a bus stop from where you can take a bus back into the centre of Leeds or return to Oakwood.

However to continue on foot, return to the gardens and go along the path with the canal on your right and exit on to Old Park Road. Turn left down Old Park Road, cross Lidgett Park Road with care and continue up hill, passing the allotments on your left.

Old Park Road is just what it says, the old road to the park estate of the Nicholsons. To the left of the road you will see playing fields and brick changing rooms for the sportsmen and women. This space was not developed when the land was being sold off after the park was established and originally formed part of the Home Farm. This is borne out with the name of one of the large houses on the left called The Homestead. Here also is Roundhay cricket and bowls club which trains many young hopefuls. Across the road to the right is Roundhay School which is now a comprehensive school but originally was a grammar school opened in 1923 designed by Fred Broadbent.

Continue down the tree lined road noticing the good views over the playing fields towards Seacroft. The fields are sometimes known as the Soldiers Fields, a reference to the fact that soldiers camped here during the first world war. On reaching a road junction turn down hill to reach Oakwood Clock where we began our walk. From here you can catch one of the many buses from the bus stop across the way, in front of the parade of shops, or retrieve your car from the car park.

Tropical World

THORNER

Start: The Mexborough Arms.   Map: OS SE 24/34
Transport: Bus from Leeds 760.
Car Parking: On the street.
Description: Country lanes and field paths. Could be muddy.
WALK A: Approximately 6km. 4 miles 2 hours.

Thorner village lies on the northern outskirts of Leeds. The history of
the village goes back a long way and it was probably in existence
before the Norman Conquest. The name suggests that it was fortified in
some way, probably by a thick thorn hedge. Many places in Yorkshire
incorporate the name Thorn(er) The village was most likely developed
because of the presence of limestone in the area. It was not good enough

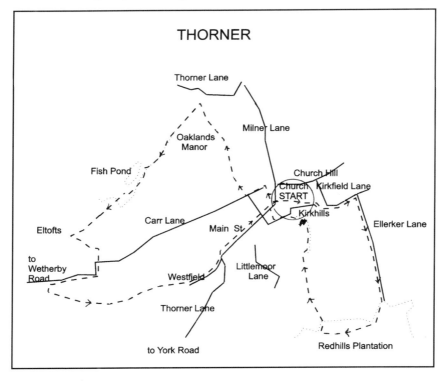

11

for building houses but when burnt provided a fertiliser for the land, and could be traded for other goods. Farming was always important, particularly sheep both for meat and wool. Linen weaving came later, the cloth being sent to Knaresborough for distribution. The Mexborough Arms, situated at the corner of Carr Lane and Main Street commerates the name of one of the influential land owners of the area.

Start the walk by going left from the Mexborough Arms along Main Street towards the Church.

Note the old school building at the bottom of the Church steps. High up on the left of the wall of the old school can be seen the date of 1766 indicating that formal education has been provided to Thorner children for many years. The lych gate too is worthy of note. The position of the Church on a hill looking down the village main street is important.

Thorner Church and Main Street

Walk on the road to the left for a short distance and turn left down a small ginnel known locally as Sam Sykes lane which continues on past the houses with a hedge on the right and an obvious banking on the left.

Just a few yards down the ginnel there used to be a well known as St.Osyth Well. Very little water is left to be seen in the summer drought, but it does still flood the lane in the wet season. The iron support for the pump is still attached to the wall. Who was Sam Sykes? Maybe he was the land owner at one time or the person responsible for maintaining the well in days gone by ?

The path goes round to the right. Continue, and go under the old railway bridge to reach Carr Lane. Walk up the lane to the Victory Hall on the right.

The Victory Hall was built by the local people in 1924 to commemorate those from Thorner and district who died in the 1914 - 18 war. It is used for many local events.

Turn right just before the hall along a roughly surfaced road. Follow the yellow arrows through a gate into a field and keep alongside the hedge on your right. Go through another gate into a large field (possibly with horses) and up the hill keeping slightly left to reach Oaklands Manor on the left. Cross the stile in the hedge into the track alongside the Manor House. Turn right along this track to bring you to the front of the Manor Lodges, East and West, and the imposing gates into the Manor House proper on the left.

Oaklands Manor, Scarcroft, is now owned by a business, but in the early part of this century it was lived in by one of the Mayors of Leeds, Albert Braithwaite, who started life as a quarry worker but later owned several brickworks.

Continue left on the road leaving Oaklands Manor and Lodge houses behind you. On leaving the complex a more wooded area now develops. Keep to the central wooded lane ignoring tracks to the left and right. You are now walking on a very pleasant country path. Keep on this same path ignoring a turn to the left through a fence, till you come to a small lake with a picnic site. This is a private lake stocked with fish. A good place to make a stop. Continue up the left hand side of the lake. With your back to the lake take a half turn to the right on a more indistinct path through a heavily wooded area. Do not turn either left or right until you reach a gate in the fence. Go through into a large field. This may have a crop, so take care to stick to the path keeping to the upper part of the field. Soon you should be able to see a group of houses on the hill to the left with a yellow marker pointing the way to go over a stile and on to the road in front of the area known as Eltofts.

Eltofts is a very ancient settlement, the name probably means Ellas enclosure. It was once part of the Earl of Mexboroughs estate and in the 1920s it was the home of Thomas Mylchreest, commemorated in Thorner Parish Church. During the 1960s the main house was home to the Catholic Bishop of Leeds. Many of the houses have been renovated, and the large house split up. All the dwellings look attractive with pleasant views towards Scarcroft.

Turn left up the lane which becomes walled on both sides for a short distance and then wooded. At a distinct corner ignore the waymarked footpath off to the left and follow the lane round to the right to join the Thorner -Shadwell road (Carr Lane). Turn right for about a quarter of a mile (take great care as this road can be busy and has sharp bends) and turn left on the waymarked footpath across the fields. Notice Birkby Grange on the hill. Cross the stile to your left and follow the field paths back towards Carr Farm. Climb the stile into the farm road and turn left. Almost immediately turn right over another stile up hill. Cross another stile and head diagonally left on an obvious field path to Westfield. In the distance can be seen the public house The Beehive. Pass by the attractively named Honeysuckle Cottage to rejoin the main road into Thorner, crossing Mill Beck, which was a ford but now has a pedestrian causeway. Continue on through the village, noticing the various styles of houses on the village street and the new houses built behind, to reach our starting point The Mexborough Arms. Perhaps a convenient stopping place for refreshments.

Start: The Mexborough Arms. Map: OS SE 24/34 and SE 23/33
Transport: Bus from Leeds 760.
Car Parking: On the street.
Description: Field and woodland paths.
WALK B: Approximately 3 km. 2 miles 1 hour.

Start the walk from the Mexborough Arms. Walk up Main Street towards the Church. Cross the road towards the Church and go through the lych gate.

Notice the old school on the right, now a private residence, and the date stone 1766 on the wall high on the left side of the building. The lych gate which adds a nice feature to the entrance to the Churchyard was added in 1935 in memory of E.B. Nussey. Take a few minutes to walk round the Churchyard noticing the names of local people buried here. The Church is well worth a look inside, particularly look at the parish chest which must have lots of stories to tell.

It is likely that there has been a Christian community existing here since the coming of Paulinus in the 7th century. There are definite records of the re-building of the church in the 15th century. Inside the Church there is a rather unusual benefaction board, which records various bequests to Thorner. Of particular relevance is that of Matthew Dodgson's bequest to the poor of Thorner, Shadwell and Scarcroft for ever. This walk passes the field which he bequeathed.

Leave the Churchyard at the top of the hill, after taking a moment to turn round and look at Thorner from this vantage point. Walk straight forward through some new houses built in 1967, bearing right at the end to see the new school erected in 1971. Keep straight on through relatively new houses, and, when the metalled road stops, take the right turn (ignore the more obvious path straight ahead) on a rough road with hedges on both sides. After about a quarter of a mile look for the inscribed stone on your left.

This stone is important in the development of the village. It tells of the generosity of Matthew Dodgson who left a large piece of land off

Ellercar Lane and a house and garden for the support of the poor of the parish in the 18th century. The charity continues to function.

Continue on the lane till you reach the wood. Take the path along the hedgeside to the right which is well walked and enters the wood. Very soon after entering the wood take the right turn, ignoring the yellow marker to the left, go over a small wooden bridge crossing a small stream to the right. In a short time follow a path to the right going quite near the edge of the wood. This path soon joins an old lane going to the right. There are remains of walls along this path and it is quite distinct. Notice the height of this field compared to the one to the right. Was this a sunken lane or merely the course of a stream? Climb over a stile in front of the gardens to nearby houses. Turn

Matthew Dodgson Stone

left and then right to return to Hall Garth open green and the Mexborough Arms.

If time permits, enjoy a look round the village, and visit the Village Green and Cross.

Village Green and Cross

BRAMHOPE

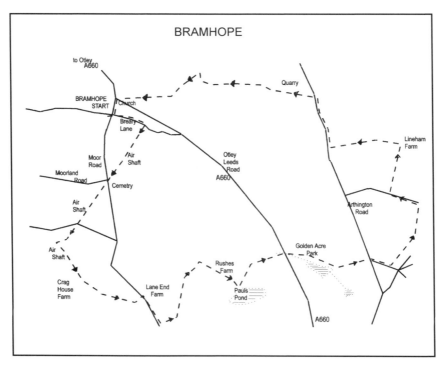

Bramhope Cross

BRAMHOPE

Start: Fox & Hounds, Bramhope.   Map: OS SE 24/34
Transport: Bus 780, 784, X82, X84
Car Parking: Old Lane, Near Fox & Hounds.
Description: Country walk, mostly flat, can be muddy.
Approximately 13km. 8 miles 4 hours.

From the bus stop make your way to the Fox & Hounds.

> *The name "Bramhope" means the place of the shrub, broom, in the narrow valley.*

From the car park on Old Lane - just behind the Fox & Hounds, walk down to the cross roads.

> *The Cross in the middle of the cross roads carries a plaque which says "This cross and lantern were presented to the village of Bramhope in 1937 by the late W. B. Woodhouse Esq." There is another small plaque "To commemorate Councillor Joe Thompson, a good servant of Bramhope." Tradition has it that there was an old elm tree on this site, which is the historic centre of the community. In the 17th Century the house at the corner of Eastgate and Moor Road was a blacksmith's smithy, and also the site of a weigh bridge until 1939.*

Cross over with care, and walk down Eastgate and Breary Lane for about 300 metres to reach a short parade of shops. Turn right on the footpath at the far end of this parade.

> *As you walk down Eastgate/Breary Lane you pass some old houses, the Weavers Cottages, and the site of the 1790 School and Town Hall, now a War Memorial.*

After 300 metres the footpath meets a road in a small housing estate. Cross the road and continue on the footpath. After 50 metres go down the stone steps on the left, then follow the path to the right. The footpath more or less follows the line of the railway tunnel, and in 500 metres the footpath passes a large stone ventilation shaft. Shortly after this it reaches Moor Road.

You pass three ventilation shafts on this walk, about 240 feet deep, to the tunnel which is part of the Leeds - Thirsk railway line which was built 1845 to 1849. There is a memorial in Otley Parish Churchyard to the 30 people who were killed during the construction of this tunnel.

Turn left on Moor Road, and about 10 metres past the junction with Moorland Road turn right on the footpath diagonally across the field, passing an old chimney on your right, more or less following the line of the overhead power cables. After about 100 metres cross a second stile, continue half left across this narrow field to go between the gorse bushes to a third stile, continue in the same direction for about 75 metres to a fourth stile. The footpath ahead passes a second stone ventilation shaft on your left. Cross over yet another stile, and continue with a small wood on your right to reach Otley Old Road. Cross slightly to the right and follow the path between two fences along the edge of the fields. At the end cross the stone stile on your left, and turn right along the bottom of the field to join a grassy lane. Turn left on this lane and pass the third ventilation shaft about 20 metres to your right.

The grass track soon becomes a narrow footpath along the right edge of the field, heading towards Cookridge communications tower.

You can see Yeadon Airport on your right. The airport was started as a flying club for enthusiasts in the 1930's. During the last war Lancaster Bombers were built at Yeadon. Today the airport is very successful with business and holiday traffic.

Just past Crag House Farm cross the stone stile in to the lane at a right hand bend. Turn left and immediately cross another stone stile on to the footpath with a wire fence on your left and a stone wall on your right. Keep ahead to a T junction near some houses. Turn left on the footpath to join Cookridge Lane opposite Lane End Farm.

Crag House Farm is used as a day centre by a Christian Association to rehabilitate youngsters.

Monument to Tunnel Builders

Turn right on Cookridge Lane for 400 metres, then left along Pinfold Lane - this is a tarmac surfaced road which passes a brick built Scout Hut and reaches a small group of houses and farm buildings. The tarmac surface now ceases, but the lane continues. After 100 metres go over a stile and keep ahead. After a further 100 metres to the next field corner, turn right with a fence on your left, passing the derelict Rushes Farm on your left to reach the wood. Go half right through the wood to reach Paul's Pond.

As you walk down Pinfold Lane you can see Cookridge Hall to your right. This is now a country club, leisure centre and golf club. Paul's Pond, probably called after a Mr. Paul from Cookridge, is a popular venue for fishermen.

The path goes to the left from the North East corner of the pond, and goes through the wood to reach the duck boards across the boggy ground, leading to the tunnel under Otley Road in to Golden Acre Park.

Golden Acre Park was opened in 1932 with a lake half a mile long and a quarter of a mile wide, with motor boats, rowing boats canoes and yachts. There was a miniature railway a mile and a half long with two locomotives. In the centre of the lake was a music tower from which music and announcements were broadcast and could be relayed to other parts of the park. The Winter Gardens was said to have the largest dance floor in Yorkshire, and the Blue Lagoon open air swimming pool was popular until 1965.

Golden Acre Park

Go all the way through the park with the lake on your right to reach a small gate near an old stone bridge. Go through the gate and turn left on the wide track leading to Arthington Road. Go straight across the road and up the tarmac surface road straight ahead leading towards Five Lane Ends. At the top of the rise, about 50 metres before the road junctions, turn left on the footpath leading to the left edge of the wood.

From Black Hill Lane you can look over towards Eccup Reservoir, one of the main water supplies for Leeds.

Turn left on Black Hill Lane (tarmac surface) for 300 metres, then right in to Swan Lane (rough surface). Just before Lineham Farm the footpath goes left, and across three fields for 500 metres to reach Arthington Road. Turn right on the road, pass the junction to Bank Top Farm on the right, and after a further 100 metres turn left on the footpath with the quarry on your right.

The quarry is in use, and there may be warnings about blasting in progress.

At the road junction just below Wood Top Farm turn right down Creskeld Lane for 100 metres, then left on to the wide bridle track going through the woods and the housing estate up to the Otley Road. The bridle track is waymarked. When it reaches the houses at the bottom of the valley it goes straight across the first road, slightly to the right at the second road, and follows the third road round to the right for 50 metres to a sharp left hand bend, where the bridle track branches off to the right, and leads up to the main Otley Road opposite to the Parish Church of St. Giles.

Just before reaching the main road is the Old Bramhope Township Well and Pump complex. The plaque says that the origins are unknown, a forgotten past is gone forever. You may use your own imagination for the story to be told by these old stones which stand on this ancient bridle path. The milestone across the road is also interesting, showing the distances in miles and furlongs to Adel School, Headingley Church, Woodhouse Moor, Leeds Bridge, and your destination, Bramhope Cross, one furlong.

Cross the road with great care, go up Church Hill with the Church on your left to reach the cross roads and the Fox & Hounds, and the car park behind it.

The Church of St. Giles was built in 1876 on part of the Rhodes Estate with stone from the Otley Chevin quarries. The Fox & Hounds is an 18th Century hostelry with an interesting lintel over the door showing "1758 T.N.B."

The Well

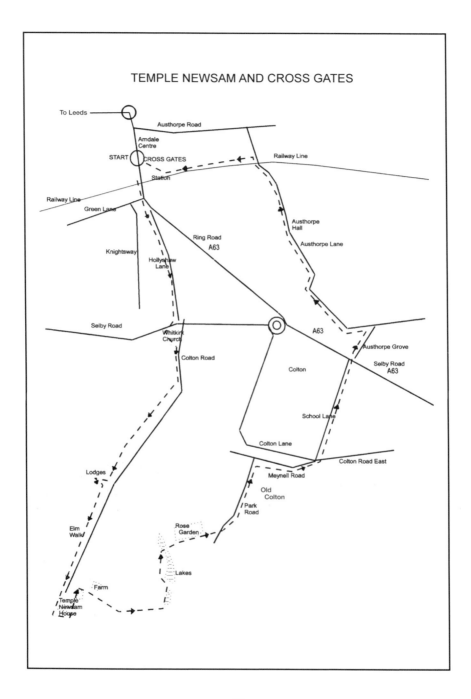

TEMPLE NEWSAM AND CROSS GATES

To Leeds

Austhorpe Road

Arndale Centre

START CROSS GATES

Railway Line

Station

Railway Line

Green Lane

Austhorpe Hall

Ring Road
A63

Austhorpe Lane

Knightsway

Hollyshaw Lane

Selby Road

Whitkirk Church

A63

Austhorpe Grove

Colton Road

Selby Road
A63

Colton

School Lane

Colton Lane

Colton Road East

Lodges

Meynell Road

Old Colton

Park Road

Elm Walk

Rose Garden

Lakes

Farm

Temple Newsam House

TEMPLE NEWSAM AND CROSS GATES

Start: Crossgates Shopping Centre.   Map: OS SE 23/33
Transport: Bus from Leeds 56, 57, 164 and 166 or Train.
Car Parking: Behind the Shopping Centre.
Description: This is a short walk through suburban streets and the park. It is short enough to enable the walker to take time to visit Temple Newsam House and Gardens, and for a visit to Home Farm to enjoy the special features provided for children.
Approximately 8 km. 5 miles 2 1/2 hours

Start the walk from Crossgates shopping centre. Cross the dual carriage way carefully taking the pedestrian crossing to the left. When you have crossed the road continue going left and take the road up hill to the right called

House at Whitkirk

Hollyshaw Lane, passing large stone houses on the right and smaller, newer, brick houses on the left. As you near the top of the hill you will see a green space on your left. This was probably where a coal mine was formerly. There were many mines in this area during the last century. Continue up to the cross roads and traffic lights.

Across the road to the left can be seen two old houses the one next to the corner house has a stone on the wall bearing a Knights Templar cross, initials and date. T W 1744.

Cross the road at the crossing towards the Church of Whitkirk. The name probably referred to the appearance of the Church when first built. Go through the lych gate into the Churchyard. If you are lucky and the Church is open it is well worth spending a few minutes looking inside. In the Churchyard are the remains of a cross.

The Church, built in the 15th century, contains some notable memorials to important local people including John Smeaton a famous engineer, noted particularly for designing the first Eddystone lighthouse that could withstand the elements. The lighthouse was removed after 120 years and re-erected on Plymouth Hoe. Other memorials in the church are to the various owners of Temple Newsam house.

Leave the Churchyard by the small gate that leads on to Colton Road and turn right. There are several interesting houses nearby including The Manor House and opposite to it The Coach House. Both the buildings probably date from the 15th century. Keep straight on the road and soon you will be surrounded by fields. Take the tarmac path through the fields on your right, parallel with the road, leading slightly up hill towards the impressive brick gateways. Do not go through the gateways. Turn right alongside the brick wall and take the first gap in the wall leading to a small car park. Straight ahead you will see a tree lined avenue (Elm Walk). Go along Elm Walk until you come to Temple Newsam House. At the end of the walk, on the left, is a very ancient tree with gnarled trunk.

Temple Newsam House and grounds (917 acres) is now owned by Leeds City Council who bought the estate in 1922. The History of the house goes back a long way and it would be well worth spending an

Temple Newsam House

hour or two discovering some of it. It is a treasure house of 18th Century furniture (Thomas Chippendale) and Leeds Pottery. You learn the amazing story of how the house was built and developed down through hundreds of years and of the people who lived there, including it's Royal connection. Lord Darnley, the father of the future King James the first, was born here 1545. However one of the most important owners and developers of the house was Sir Arthur Ingram a 17th Century wheeler and dealer who is said to have been so wealthy that he even lent money to Charles 1.

Go straight ahead and walk round the outside of the house anti - clockwise, with the house on your left. You can enjoy seeing the gardens, and admire the view over the estate from the side where you can see the house built round three sides of an open square. The central part of the Western front is early Tudor with Jacobean corners but the South front is Georgian. Looking up the balustrade catches ones eye. The lettering was originally put up in stone but was replaced by metal in 1788.

"All glory and praise be given to God the Father the Son and Holy Ghost on high peace on earth good will towards men honour and true allegiance to our gracious King loving affection amongst his subjects health and plenty be within this house". Probably this inscription was erected to make a point of the loyalty of the then owner of the house Sir Arthur Ingram, as the loyalty of previous owners had been in question. The rainwater pipes are also decorated, by later owners, with coronets, cockerels, scallop shells etc. The brick work is also in an interesting pattern.

Continue ahead to the stable block. (Turning left would bring you to the entrance of the House.) In the stable block are a cafe, toilets and information.

Go down the tarmac path towards Home Farm and keep to the right hand path down to a small lake.

There are many old and rare trees to be admired. In May and June there is a magnificent display of rhodendrons and azalea. Notice some unusual gates to the left with sphinx on the tops.

Turn left on the tarmac path with the lake on your right, at the head of the lake turn left up hill and follow round to the right with a second small lake on your right. Cross the bridge over the stream at the head of this second small lake, turn right on the footpath for a few metres, then take the first footpath on your left which goes between some derelict red brick buildings. This leads up a slope to leave the grounds of Temple Newsam by an unusual metal gateway designed to be easily opened by people on horseback.

You are now walking on a hard surface through a field, to the left can be seen a large farm complex, Colton Farm. On leaving the field and negotiating another metal barrier you can admire the old red brick farm buildings. If you look backwards you will see the large glass houses that belong to Temple Newsam estate and the rose gardens. Go up the road (Park Road) leading towards the old village of Colton, passing several old houses and an old mill stone built in to the wall of Sycamore House. At the cross roads turn right on Meynell Road (reference to the last owners of Temple Newsam) this passes Colton Village Institute, a wooden building, on the left and ends with concrete bollards. The footpath continues to join Colton Lane nearly opposite old Colton school. Cross Colton Lane and walk along School Lane, noticing Colton Institute and its cricket ground, and the new housing estate across the road appropriately called The Wickets. Keep straight on and you will pass the shopping centre, Sainsburys, on the right. On reaching the Selby Road, dual carriage way, cross using the pedestrian crossing (next to the crossing specially for horses). Turn right briefly and then left on to Austhorpe Grove going through a housing estate. At the next T junction turn left on Barrowby Lane. You will soon pass Austhorpe school on the right. Down the hill from here once stood Austhorpe Lodge where John Smeaton was born.

The house where John Smeaton, engineer, was born in 1724 was pulled down some years ago. It must have been a very interesting house, where he worked on many of his projects. There was a forge and a work room, and it is a shame that there is nothing to be seen there now. Smeaton, as well as being responsible for the Eddystone lighthouse, also worked on the canals that were transforming the face of England in the 18th century. He contributed much to the term Civil Engineer which had not previously been recognised in that century.

At the next junction keep right and at the top of the next rise can be seen Austhorpe House built in 1694. This is a lovely red brick house with stone coinstones. Probably the presence of so many brick houses in the area is evidence of the good clay available for brick making before the coal beds were reached. Keep on this road and on the right across the fields will be seen large modern buildings which house the Barn Bow armaments factory owned by Vickers. You will soon reach a railway bridge, cross this using the pedestrian pavement on the left. Straight forward can be seen the Manston public house. Our way however (unless you are in need of refreshments) takes us to the left along a narrow road way parallel with the railway on the left. Soon a smaller path takes you even nearer to the railway cutting and passes the old gas holder to reach the shopping centre at Crossgates. From here you can return to Leeds either by bus or train.

Austhorpe House 1694

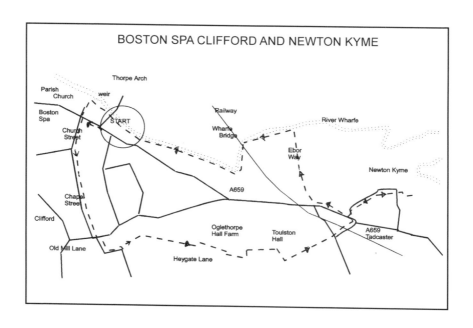

BOSTON SPA CLIFFORD AND NEWTON KYME

Royal Hotel

BOSTON SPA, CLIFFORD, NEWTON KYME

Start: Boston Spa.   Map: OS sheet SE 44/54

Transport: 760 Wetherby bus from Leeds bus station.

Car Park: In the village near the cross roads. There are no yellow lines on the road so it may also be possible to park on the street.

Description: A walk along well defined paths, returning along the Ebor way beside river Wharfe.

Approximately 9kms 5 1/2 miles 3 hours plus a 1km diversion to Newton Kyme.

The walk starts from the Royal Hotel near the centre of Boston Spa.

The Royal Hotel, The Crown and the Admiral Hawke were all built in the late 1700s to help look after the growing numbers of visitors coming to the area to partake of the spa waters. The waters which eventually gave the name to the area were discovered in 1774 by a local man called John Shires. He was out one day cutting brushwood to thatch a house when he discovered a spring flowing down the bank in the area known as Ox Close, near the river Wharfe. The area was then in the village of Clifford. This water was proved to be beneficial for its purgative and diuretic powers. The taking of these waters became popular and the place became known as Thorpe Arch Spa (just across the river) for a time. But later the name was changed to Boston Spa - maybe from the Latin for ox - bos and the Saxon for township ton.

Walk along the pavement towards the Parish Church and turn left along Church Street.

Continue down this road on the pavement noticing many large stone houses along the way. A house on the left is now a small school, St. Vincents. Soon the pavement on the left ends and it is advisable to cross the road and join the pavement on the right there. Notice a large house on the right called Croft House, outside this house a rubbish bin has been provided by the people in Croft House. A nice gesture. Continue going up hill now, the road becomes

Chapel Street. You may remember it started as Church Street. At the top of a slight rise you can see a large Church ahead of you and you will pass The Vicarage on your way to this Church. The imposing Church is the Catholic Church dedicated to St. Edward.

> *The Church is not very old but is built in the Norman style. St Edward was King of England in the 11th Century and became known as The Confessor. The massive tower can be seen for miles around and has three open arches. The Church is very light and airy inside because of the large windows. There is a statue of the Madonna inside.*

It would be very pleasant to spend some time looking round Clifford, turning to the right to reach the War Memorial and also another Church. There are some beautiful old houses and typical village shops to be explored if time permits.

Return to the Catholic Church and continue with the walk. Notice an old tower across from the Church.

At the corner of the Church turn left and very soon you will meet Old Mill Lane. Turn right down this lane and past some new houses, the road curves left to reach the Old Wheel House on the left. In fact the old wheel is still there inside a rusting casement by the side of the house. Continue, the road now curving right, uphill. After the last house go into the lane which turns to the left behind the houses. Take the waymarked Public Footpath which becomes a very pleasant path through a large field with a fence on one side and a hedge on the other. Ignore a stile to the left and continue on the path.

> *You now get very good views all-round. To the right on a hill can be seen the remains of a windmill, to the left in the far distance can be seen the British Library at Thorp Arch.*
> *Looking back you also get good views of Clifford.*

Continue on the path as before, the hedge and fence eventually disappear and you come to a T junction. This is Heygate Lane. The path is now surfaced. Take the turning to the left and then a turning to the right and it becomes a green track going towards a large farm. There may be an electric fence on the left. Soon another T junction will be reached. Take the right turn this time and very soon a stile will be seen on the left. Go over this stile, you can see the large farm now on your left. This is Ogelthorpe Hall Farm. The path comes to a right turn by a farm gate and continues through the fields with a ditch on your left. Go through a small copse signed towards Toulston. Soon you will pass Toulston Hall on your left. Keep on the path which makes a zig zag and then passes alongside a pond. You will pass through several farm buildings, worth a photograph, and then you will come to a cross roads. You can see an old railway bridge straight forward and some red brick buildings. Go straight forward under the railway bridge.

This bridge is part of the redundant Wetherby to Tadcaster railway line. The road to the right that we ignored at the cross road is said to be an old Roman Road known as Rudgate.

After going under the bridge continue on to the A659 Tadcaster road. On reaching the road turn left and cross the road with care. Almost immediately you will see the minor road to Newton Kyme going off to the right It is well worth taking this diversion to Newton Kyme if time permits. Take this road towards the village. You will pass a sign on the left towards St Helens Well.

St Helen is always associated with the Romans and was said to be Constantine's mother. As Newton Kyme is very near Tadcaster (Roman town of Calcaria) it is quite likely that this well was known to the Romans.

Continue along this country road passing two junctions till you reach a small green island in the middle of the road with a sundial in the centre. Watch out for a sign on the right "To the Church and the Ebor Way." Take this short path through the field to the Church. You will get a good view of Newton Kyme Hall on the left.

Newton Kyme village is dominated by several very large houses, particularly Newton Kyme Hall and The Dower House. The Hall is sited alongside the River Wharfe with parkland and lawns protected from the possibility of animals straying into the garden by a Ha-Ha. The Hall is said to date from the 17th Century and has a colonnaded balcony on its frontage.

Admiral Robert Fairfax was born here in 1666 and he restored the house of an earlier date and planted many noble trees in the grounds. The Admiral died in 1725 and is buried inside the Church. It is thought

Newton Kyme Hall

that the way from the Church to the main road used to pass through a grand avenue of limes with no doubt imposing gateways. But because of the Fairfax's part on the side of Cromwell during the Civil War these gateways were removed by Charles 11's decree. The Church, which probably dates from 12th Century, has some interesting features and is dedicated to St Andrew. There is a squint opening towards the altar. The Churchyard has also some interesting things including an unusual free standing arch, two graves, one with no name but adorned with a large cross carved in the stone, the other is made of brick with RUTH picked out and the date 1895-1915. She was Ruth Bethell who died young and was obviously much loved.

The village is worth a look round before returning to the A695. Turn right noticing the old mile stone across the way. After about five minutes you reach a road coming in from the left and a path turning off to the right. Turn

Newton Kyme Churchyard

right on the path. This is the continuation of Rudgate (the old Roman Road). It will eventually bring you to the bank of the River Wharfe. The path becomes quite small but is still clear and is part of The Ebor Way from York to Ilkley. Looking across the river it is possible to think of the Romans fording the river here in the summer and visiting St.Helens well. Turn to the left and walk along the river bank on the Ebor Way towards Boston Spa.

The path is interesting all along the river bank with wild fowl, old willow trees and fishermen etc. Across the river can also be seen Thorpe Arch trading estate.

Continue along the river following the twists and turns going underneath the railway bridge Wharfe Bridge. Take care as the river bank can be slippy and dangerous when the river is in flood. Keep on the Ebor way over a wooden bridge and past Papyrus Paper Mill ignoring any paths off to the left till the old Spa Bath buildings are reached on the river bank.

There are many fine Georgian houses in Boston Spa overlooking the river. The Spa was discovered in the 18th century (see beginning) and became quite important though it was never as successful as Harrogate.

At one time there was a court case about who actually owned the rights to the water and this court case probably helped the downfall of the Spa. New baths and pump rooms had been built in 1834 by R. O Gascoigne with hot and cold water.

Continue bearing right along on the river bank and go under the magnificent stone road bridge across the river which would take you to the small village of Thorpe Arch. After going under the bridge you will come to the large weir across the river which probably would at one time help to work a water wheel for a corn mill. Just before the weir take the path to the left which becomes a sunken road through the woods and up the small hill to bring you up to the main road through Boston Spa and immediately on the right is the parish Church of St Marys, built in 1814.

You can now catch a bus back to Leeds by crossing the road, the bus stop is only a few yards to the left towards the Royal, or return to the car park.

BRAMHOPE TO OTLEY

Start: The centre of Bramhope or the Parish Church.
Map: OS S/E 24/34 Harewood
Transport: Bus from Leeds Bus station Nos. X84,784,780,X82.
Car Parking: Near the Fox & Hounds in Bramhope.
Description: Pleasant rural walk, added bonus of Otley at the end.
Approximately 7km. 4 1/2 miles 2 hours.

From the car park near the Cross and the Fox & Hounds walk down hill to
the left to the Cross (more properly the light in the middle of the road now)
turn left down the steep hill to the Parish Church of St. Giles. It is worth
spending a few minutes looking at the mile-stone on the corner which names
some places round about and the distances in miles and furlongs. The Cross
for instance is a furlong away up the hill we have just come down.
Alternatively if you have come by bus have a look at the stone before
crossing the road. Cross the Leeds - Otley road carefully. Walk on the

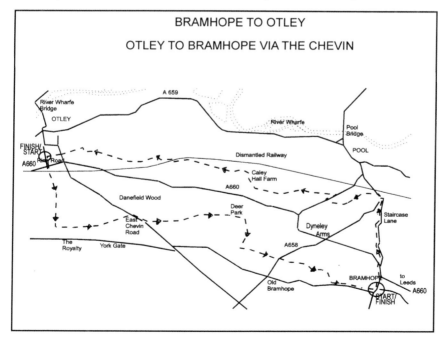

pavement towards the Bramhope Post House, pass the Post House and notice the old Puritan Chapel. Spare a thought for the people who built it in Cromwellian times. This Chapel is normally closed but I believe it is open from 10 a.m. to 4 p.m. on Sundays - April to October or the key is available at the Post House if you are particularly interested in the Chapel. Continue on the road for a few yards and you come to a small cross roads. Take the left of the two lanes, called Staircase Lane. Go down hill passing several old houses including Staircase House. The path now becomes muddy and not suitable for vehicles. Continue down hill. You come to a large house which looks private. They seem to have constructed a "by pass" footpath going round the garden to the left. Take this well graded path uphill. This path rejoins the path that comes directly from the large house and both paths go to the left towards the road. There is a large stone house at the corner of the road and the path called Firs Hill Court. Turn right on the road for a few metres then cross over, being very careful as it is a very busy road. Go through the imposing arched gateway called Avenue des Hirondelles. (The Avenue of the Swallows)

The story goes that the avenue was first developed by a publican, hence the swallow, a play on drinking. May be just a joke.

Turn up the Avenue which is very pleasantly lined with chestnut trees. The large houses have good views over Wharfedale, certainly in the winter. Keep on up hill. After the last of the houses the avenue of trees continues but your

Church Lane

The Smithy at Bramhope

path turns slightly down hill to enter a wood. Turn right. Go over the stile down hill. Notice the views over Wharfedale, of Pool and the large red brick paper works in the valley next to the river. You are along-side an old wall and soon go past what once could have been a stone bridge. On the right over the wall can be seen a large stone house with extensive gardens and a Union Jack flying. Continue on your path and soon you will pass a small row of stone half Tudor cottages on your left called Sandy Lobby. On reaching a tarmac road turn right down hill, passing Overdale Manor on your right, the large house previously mentioned, with very well maintained walls and hedges.

Almost opposite Overdale Manor there is a small stile in the stone wall, and a gate. Cross the stile and turn almost back on yourself going through a field with the wall on your right. Keep on to another stile, cross over and continue till you come to a walled lane. You will now be passing a farm on either side. The large modern barn on the right is part of Caley Hall Farm. Cross the farm road and immediately across you will see a public footpath marked to Otley. Take this path through a small field (this field had Alpacas in December 1997). Cross over another stile noticing the sign warning that when the Highland cattle in the field have young they must be avoided. Skirt round this field on the path near the fence. You will soon come to a road which leads to Caley Hall. Cross this road and climb the iron stile into another field.

The Well at Otley

Go through several fields following the yellow markers through and over several stiles. Eventually you will meet a path which goes towards the old railway line and a small copse of silver birches. Turn left and walk parallel with the old railway line going through stiles, some of which are rather rickety so take care. Ignore an old railway bridge and continue on following the markers till you come to a larger railway bridge .You will come to a small stream and the path turns sharp right over yet another difficult stile under an old railway bridge. Just after going under this bridge the path goes to the left through a thorny patch (could be overgrown in the summer). Follow this path which bends to the right. At a small wooden seat take the public footpath to the left through a kissing gate. Keep on the path through large fields towards Otley.

> *These fields are known locally as the Irish fields. Whether this is a reference to Irish immigrants camping here, perhaps working on the railway, or is a corruption of Iris fields is not certain.*

Keep on the same line till you go across a large field, there is a chimney straight forward, and modern houses just on the edge of the field. You pass through a kissing gate on to a surfaced path, turn right here. Soon you will come to a small estate of pleasant houses. Keep going right. This is Peterhouse Drive. You soon reach a T junction and turn right, passing Kings Close on your left. Keep on Cambridge Drive, Cambridge Way, Cambridge Grove, until you meet two large terraces of stone houses, and in a short time a public footpath is seen on the right. Take this path through modern houses till a left hand turn brings you to stone sett road to the left. This brings you into Otley, a large garage on the left, a cycle shop and several public houses on Bondgate to the right. You are now in Otley.

Otley is a very pleasant market town with many attractions. There are lots of places to eat and drink. Market days are Friday and Saturday when the town streets are filled with colourful stalls and the atmosphere is very lively. It is worth having a walk round to look at the Parish Church; the statue to Thomas Chippendale who was born in the town and became an accomplished furniture maker in the 18th Century; the monument to the people killed whilst building the railway line; the clock in the market place given by Belgians who stayed in the town during the 1914 -1918 war and the riverside.

The Bridge, Otley

OTLEY TO BRAMHOPE

Start: Otley Fire Station.
Transport: Bus. X84,784,780,X82.
Car Parking: In Otley near the main Post Office.
Description: Pleasant country walk steep uphill at first.
Approximately 7km. 4 1/2 miles 3 hours.

Map OS SE 24/34 Harewood

Walk on Bondgate passing the Fire Station and the Qwick-Fit Garage on
your right. Turn right at the footpath sign pointing through the ginnel
towards the Chevin. After about a hundred yards you will come to small
modern bungalows. Turn right here to come to a street of large terrace
houses. Turn left to walk past the terrace houses to the top of the street, which
is blocked off to traffic. You come to the site of the old railway station. Cross
the modern metal bridge over Otley by-pass. Continue uphill on the path past
a small farm. On reaching a road take the footpath straight opposite. There

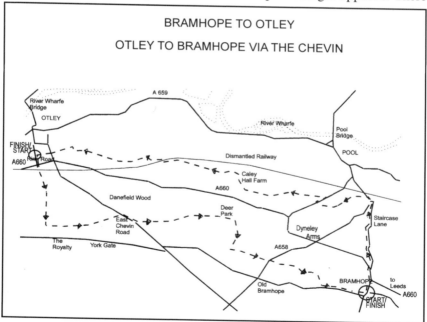

BRAMHOPE TO OTLEY

OTLEY TO BRAMHOPE VIA THE CHEVIN

are large stone gateposts to the right - The Old Vicarage. The footpath is called Yorkgate. Keep going up the steep stone stepped path, passing a white building on your right which once housed a small spa and now is a field centre. This is not on our path but can be visited some times in the summer. Eventually a grassy path takes you to the top of the Chevin, approximately 800ft above sea level.

Just before reaching the top of the Chevin you will see a carved wooden figure that looks like a monk reading a book. Unfortunately there is no notice board explaining who did the carving or why it is here. On the right you may also see an old stone fence, called a vaccary wall, which is said to be an ancient wall erected to keep cattle from straying. Occasionally a beacon is lit on top of the Chevin at times of national rejoicing. At Easter the local people put a cross on this obvious high point. Pause to admire the view of Otley and pick out various beauty spots like Almscliff Crag to the right, Norwood Edge to the North, the flooded gravel pits in the valley, now used by bird watchers and for other leisure activities.

Turn left along the Chevin away from Otley. You will soon pass a car park on your right, near to a famous pub called The Royalty. Keep walking along

The Clock in Otley Market Square

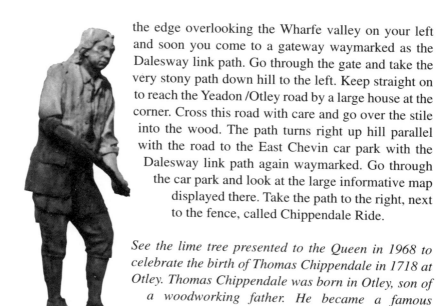

Thomas Chippendale

the edge overlooking the Wharfe valley on your left and soon you come to a gateway waymarked as the Dalesway link path. Go through the gate and take the very stony path down hill to the left. Keep straight on to reach the Yeadon /Otley road by a large house at the corner. Cross this road with care and go over the stile into the wood. The path turns right up hill parallel with the road to the East Chevin car park with the Dalesway link path again waymarked. Go through the car park and look at the large informative map displayed there. Take the path to the right, next to the fence, called Chippendale Ride.

See the lime tree presented to the Queen in 1968 to celebrate the birth of Thomas Chippendale in 1718 at Otley. Thomas Chippendale was born in Otley, son of a woodworking father. He became a famous furniture maker when Lord Lascelles of Harewood House commissioned him to make furniture for his new house.

Walk on this woodland path following the Dalesway link path, over a bridge, and continue for half a mile or so to reach a right turn. Turn right uphill for about two hundred yards, keeping a rather bare field on your left called Caley Deer Park. Your path goes right and is still the Dalesway link. Turn left, just before a Dalesway sign on a tree stump, in to the wood. Aim for the top left corner of the wood and cross the stile waymarked Dalesway and Ebor Way. Continue across the top of a field and then between two walls until you reach the A658 road. Turn left near Old Pool Bank top. Very soon cross the road and take the small path with a hedge on the left and a wall on the right. This wall is a boundary wall for a collection of stone buildings, which used to be a childrens home. The sign says Hilton Grange School. Redevelopment has started. Keep on through the fields until you will see the beginnings of Bramhope village appearing. You now turn right on a small lane hedged on both sides which takes you through Old Bramhope, with the cricket ground on the right and eventually on to the old school buildings, the public toilets, the Cross, the Fox & Hounds. From here it is a short walk down hill to the left to the Church and the bus stop . The A660 is the road to Leeds from where you can catch a bus either to Otley or Leeds.

Before catching a bus back to Otley or returning to Leeds notice the ancient stone by the side of the Parish Church of St. Giles. This stone tells us how far it is to several places in miles and furlongs. This must have been very useful in the past. If you are doing this walk on a Sunday you way be lucky and gain entrance into the Church. Otherwise like so many Churches now you can not appreciate its beauty from the inside.

Otley from the Chevin

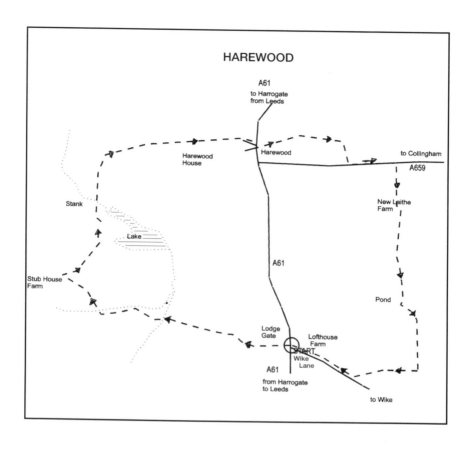

HAREWOOD

A61
to Harrogate
from Leeds

Harewood
House

Harewood

to Collingham

A659

New Laithe
Farm

Stank

Lake

Stub House
Farm

A61

Pond

Lodge
Gate

Lofthouse
Farm

START

Wike
Lane

A61

from Harrogate
to Leeds

to Wike

HAREWOOD

Start: Wike Lane End.   Map: OS SE 24/34
Transport: Bus 36 36A 36C 781 X35.
Car Parking: Wike Lane End, junction with A61
Description: Country walk through Estate land and farms on good bridle
paths and roads.
The last stretch may be muddy.
Approximately 10 km.. 6 1/2 miles 3 hours

Start the walk preferably from Wike Lane end. This is a circular walk so it is
possible to start from Harewood itself, but parking in Harewood is very
limited. If you intend to have a meal, snack or drink at the Harewood Arms
after the walk probably the landlord would give his permission to park
behind the pub. However this walk description actually starts from Wike
Lane end.

Harewood Park Gates

Rosie's Seat and Harewood House

There is room for several cars at the road side but it is popular. Cross the Leeds Harewood road taking great care as it is a busy road. Immediately across the road there are large gates with a side gate for entrance into Harewood estate on a right of way.

> *You will now enjoy a peaceful scene that is the Harewood park. The park was developed by the famous gardener known as Capability Brown for the Lascelles family in the 18th Century. The family still live at Harewood and it is due to their generosity that we can enjoy this very attractive walk at all seasons of the year. Harewood House was originally designed by John Carr of York in 1759, but was later altered and added to by Charles Barry. The present Earl is cousin to the Queen and this royal connection brings many visitors to the house including Australians as the Countess is Australian.*
>
> *You may like to visit the house yourself after the walk. The Bird Garden is especially loved by children.*

Continue on the level path through a gate and notice the ha ha on the left, probably there to keep cattle out of the woodland. You may well see lots of pheasants and other birds. There are good views of the house to the right. Continue on down hill towards the wood, go through a gate into the wood.

After 20 metres you come to a lovely stone bridge over one of the many streams on the estate. As you cross the bridge look to your left to see the waterfall. Our path takes us up stream to the left clearly waymarked as a bridle way, after 20metres fork right marked Leeds Country Way. After about a quarter of an hour walking up hill the path dips slightly to cross over a stream. On the left, over the estate wall, can be seen some new buildings that have been built for use in the television show "Emmerdale". It is possible to look over the wall to get a glimpse. You continue on the bridle way noticing many new trees planted on the left. In about ten minutes from the second stream crossing you come to some telegraph poles and a clear view down hill to the right, you should be able to see Stank and possibly, in the winter, to see through the trees the lake of Harewood estate. Just beyond the telegraph poles we come to a cross roads. The left bridle way would take you to Eccup Reservoir, you take the right turn down hill on the Ebor Way. After about 50 metres you come to a T junction, turn right again very soon continuing down hill. In about 50 metres, before reaching the field gate, turn left down the public bridle path waymarked the Ebor Way.

This footpath brings you down to Carr House farm and a large barn looking over a lovely meadow towards Harewood House on the hill straight ahead and the lake slightly to the right. Continue with the wood on your left and the meadow on your right. The path bends to the left away from the lake and then turns up the slope to the right, with a brick wall on the right. At the top end of the brick wall you come to a sign post that says The Bothy on the right. You continue on the Ebor Way, now a tarmac surfaced estate road with a stone wall on your right. Go down passing an attractive house on your left and a bridge on the right leading into the estate. Keep to the left over another small bridge You are still on the bridle way going straight ahead. Pass the farm buildings of Stank, and the conversion to business premises of Harewood Yard.

> *The name Stank probably meant a marshy place. There could be lots of water around here, the little stream passing under the bridge has a weir on it. Perhaps there was once a mill here. This stream leads to Harewood Lake to the right.*

You are now on a concrete road going up hill past more stone buildings. There is a good view over Wharfedale from the top as you now turn right on

Harewood Church

an estate road. Still going up hill through a wooded area keep your eyes open because there is a hidden delight just through a gap marked with a private entrance sign. It may be difficult to see in the summer, but in the winter you will see a small stone columned temple hidden amongst the trees. Keep on this wide estate road with a magnificent stone wall on both sides. You will now come to a broad track going off to the right. It is worth going along this for about a hundred yards to a gate closing off the entrance to Harewood Church. The Church is seldom open.

Many of the dead of the Gascoignes and the Lascelles are buried here. The more illustrious of the families are buried in the church itself. There is an amazing collection of alabaster tombs inside the Church. The oldest of the tombs is of Sir William Gascoigne who refused to sign the death warrant of Archbishop Scrope in 1405. The Gascoignes were the previous owners of what is now known as the Harewood Estate.

Continue on your original path, the estate road with walls on either side, after looking at the Churchyard. Soon, ignoring footpath signs to the left, you will come to the main Leeds/Harrogate road with The Harewood Arms public house opposite. This is a good place for lunch, coffee etc. Your path keeps to the left of the Harewood Arms along a tarmac road at first. Keep straight on the path which is parallel with the Harewood/Collingham road to the right.

You pass by a lovely pair of gates on the left leading to Maltkiln House. It must have wonderful views of Wharfedale. You pass a gas installation and the rather gaunt looking remains of a water tower on your right. There is a steep drop on the left down to the river and a farm. The farm has a rather unusual road which is in a figure of eight. This is the Harewood Hill Climb - a car racing circuit which is apparently quite challenging and draws large crowds when an event is being held. You now go through a gate and take the stile immediately to the right with a hedge on your right. This takes you along the edge of fields to come to the Harewood Collingham road. Turn left and take great care walking alongside this road for about 500metres. Traffic comes along at great speed, so be very careful and walk in single file.

You will see on your left an entrance gate to Stockton Grange Farm and the Hill Climb. Cross over the road noticing a mile stone giving distances to Wetherby etc. Turn right down the lane towards New Laithe Farm. This is a large farm with several buildings. Keep to the left of the buildings. The path is waymarked with arrows. Go a short distance on a concrete path, then through two gates and over a stream. Go through another gate, this field can be very muddy in wet weather, and into a large field. Aim for the stone buildings that can be seen on a hill. Keep to the left of Hollin Hall which has two unusual weather vanes, one of a heron and one of a fox on the roofs of the buildings. The heron is appropriate as just a little way down hill is a large pond that is used by fishermen, and is probably the happy hunting ground of herons. Leaving the pond go up hill with the wood on your left following a well marked path. Where the path appears to go down hill to the left keep straight on up hill through two gates and eventually to a large sign marking the Leeds Country Way.

Turn right here on the Country Way, ignore a path to the left which leads to various buildings. These are part of Wike village. Go through a gate and keeping the wood on your right walk on till you come to the Wike /Harewood road. Turn right and again taking care (another fast road) keep on this road passing Lofthouse Farm till Wike Lane End appears and the junction with the Leeds/Harewood Road A61. From here a bus can be taken back to Leeds, to the left, or from across the road to Harewood or Harrogate.

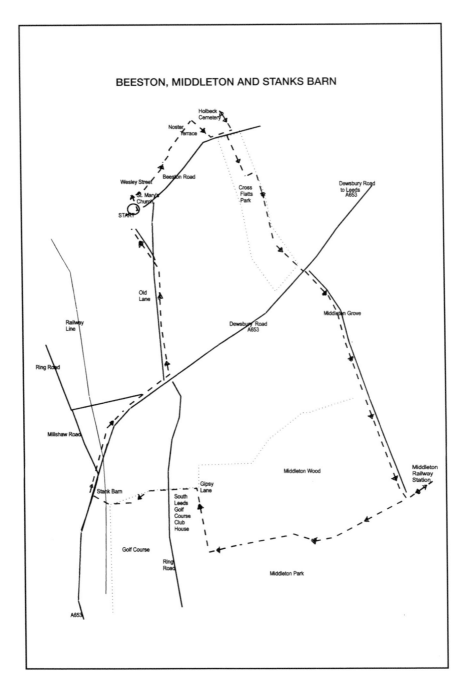

BEESTON, MIDDLETON AND STANKS BARN

BEESTON, MIDDLETON AND STANKS BARN

Start: St. Marys Church,
Beeston Road, Beeston.   Map: OS SE 23/33 and SE 22/32
Transport: Bus 93 96 96A 96C
Car Parking: Near the Cooperative Supermarket. Free.
Description: Easy walking mostly on good paths.
Approximately 8km. 5 miles 3 hours.

This is a very interesting part of Leeds with much still left on the ground
to tell us of Leeds industrial history. The walk takes us through pleasant
woodland and scenic town scape.

Start the walk at St Marys Church on Beeston Road. Facing the Church look
to the left and you should see Wesley Street going down hill. Go down this
road briefly and then take the path that contours round the Churchyard with
an old stone wall on the right. This is obviously a very old right of way and
passes by modern houses on the left. Soon the wall finishes and a chain link
fence skirts round a small estate of old peoples' bungalows.

These bungalows are on the site where there was previously a cricket
ground where many of Beeston's celebrated Carnivals were held.

Continue on to the end of the bungalows till you reach a road called
Sunnyview Gardens. Cross over this road and slightly to your left, passing a
large red brick building on your right, continue on the path which is on the
edge of a steep slope. From here you get very good views on a clear day. This
is called Beggars Hill.

From this view point looking to the left down in the valley you should
be able to see the football ground of Elland Road, further away and to
the right the Church towers of St. Lawrence, Pudsey and St.
Bartholomew's Armley. Much further to the right can be seen the
imposing white tower of the Parkinson building on the University and
slightly more to the right the well known tower of Leeds Town Hall.
Beggars Hill was once the site of a colliery and nearby a farm.

After admiring the view continue on till you have passed the terrace houses behind the red brick wall and reached a tarmac road going to the right, Noster Terrace.

Noster Terrace could possibly refer to the Monks of Kirkstall singing or saying their prayers. It is difficult to believe in these days but possibly, in earlier times, when the wind was blowing in the right direction you could have heard something of these devout men.

Turn right down Noster Terrace till you come to Beeston Road again. You have just walked past a stone wall surrounding Holbeck cemetery. Turn left again along side this wall and continue down Beeston Road till you come to an entrance into the cemetery.

Go up the steps and fork right past the war memorial. You will soon see some imposing gates on the right and a lodge house. A path to the left of this lodge, still in the cemetery, leads you to the large tomb of the Marsden family with a figure on the top reading from a book.

Many members of the family of Marsden are buried here but the most famous was Henry Rowland Marsden, J.P. Mayor of Leeds in 1874-5. Henry Rowland Marsden emigrated to America in 1848 where he made a fortune with his inventions. On his return he devoted his life to local politics becoming mayor shortly before he died.

Cad Beeston House

Return to the cemetery gates and the lodge. Keeping to the extreme left path you will see many similar grave stones of paupers in communal graves. Look over the wall to the left of these pauper graves and you will see a half timbered house known as Cad Beeston. Keep on the cemetery path which will bring you back to where you entered, on Beeston Road. From here it is worth taking a small diversion to have a look at Cad Beeston.

Turn to the left on Beeston Road and you will see a small road to the left, blocked off to traffic, turn left on this pedestrian way passing Cad Beeston Mews, till you will see a large house called Cad Beeston Manor House. It is being used as offices but you can walk round the side to see the beautiful timber work on this house built in 1421. This early date makes this building the oldest secular building in Leeds. The Regency town house on the road side partially hides the fifteenth century manor house. It is interesting to speculate on the people who have lived in this house, how it came to survive, and the unusual name. Cad may refer to an Old English name Cada, or be a corruption of cat (possibly wild cats in the area once). Certainly who ever owned the house in the past would have had a wonderful view over the Aire valley.

After admiring Cad Beeston Manor House return to Beeston Road and the entrance to the cemetery. Cross the road and you will see two large stone gate posts and the entrance into Cross Flatts Park. Walk through the park down the central path. This is a very pleasant park with flower beds and open space for children to play.

Cross Flatts Park covers 44 acres and was set out as a park in the 19th century. There used to be a bandstand, fish pond and an aviary. It is easy to imagine Beeston people congregating here on a summers evening to chat and enjoy the scenery. However a fairly new building erected in 1952 tells us of the love of Beeston kept in the hearts of emigrants to far away places. A man called Thomas Watson gave £2,000 on his return from South Africa to build this shelter. He also donated money to his old school Beeston Primary and a stained glass window to the Wesleyan Chapel.

Continue through the park till you reach Dewsbury Road. Cross this busy road using the pedestrian crossing at the traffic lights. After crossing turn left for a few metres then take the first turning to the right up Middleton Grove. Keep straight on through an industrial estate passing South Leeds Stadium on the left, and a little further on Leeds Equestrian Centre. Eventually you reach a barrier, go through this and you are now on a pleasant woodland way. Keep going uphill on a tarmac path. Enjoy the view from the top. Ignore turnings off to the right. The path eventually goes down a steep hill towards a collection of buildings through two large wooden gates. These buildings were once Middleton Broom Colliery. The last coal taken from here was in 1968. If you take a small diversion on a path to the left this will take you to the old Middleton Railway. There is also a good view of South Leeds Stadium from here.

South Leeds Stadium

The present day railway is operated by volunteers and has its main terminus in Moor Road, Hunslet. Trains run on this line from Moor Road, Hunslet to Belle Isle (Middleton Broom Colliery site) each weekend throughout the year. The history of the railway goes back to 1755 when Charles Brandling built the first railed waggonway in the area. This was to enable him to take his coal to the river Aire at Thwaite Gate. Due to Brandlings manager John Blenkinsop and the engineering skills of Matthew Murray the first commercially successful steam engine was developed.

After viewing the railway return to the site of the colliery and the road. Go across the road and through between the large stone gate posts which mark

Stanks Barn

the Belle Isle entrance into Middleton Woods. Take the central path through the wood which has a hard surface and goes slightly up hill. To the left of the path down the slope can be seen a small stream. If you look carefully you will probably see small bell pits (hollowed out shapes) where coal and iron were extracted in the past. In the winter through the trees to the right you will be able to see a grassy area known as The Clearings. In spring there are many bluebells.

> *Much of this area would have had its trees cut down for use at the colliery, pit props etc. and the oak bark used for local tanning trade. Later the area was used for entertainment. In 1932 there was a visit of Alan Cobhams Flying Circus. Unfortunately this lead to a tragic accident when two children were killed by a taxiing aircraft. In the last war searchlights were set up on the Clearings and there was also a prisoner of war camp.*

Keep on the original path which continues up hill. Through trees to the left you may be able to see golfers. Turn off to the right by a black iron gatepost on the path going steeply down hill to join another path continuing to the left uphill. After about 150yds you should come to cross paths. Turn right on the clear path down hill to South Leeds Golf Clubhouse.

To the left of this path can be seen a sunken path known locally as Gipsy Lane, to the left of Gipsy Lane is yet another way flagged (ancient causeway) This path is called Balkcliffe Lane.

Pass the club house and continue on a hard surface to reach a footpath sign on the left "Public Footpath to Stanks Farm Barn". Turn left on this path and follow the yellow markers which lead to steps going down to Beeston Ring Road. Cross this busy road with care, and ascend the steps up the opposite bank, waymarked as a public footpath.

Follow this marked path which follows round the boundary of the golf course. The path eventually goes down hill to go through a chain link fence to the left of some blocks of flats. Keep to the left of the flats, the path goes through another fence to reach a hard path going down hill to a railway bridge. Cross this bridge and you are at Stanks Hall and Barn.

Stanks Barn has fairly recently been restored and it now represents quite an asset to the area. At the time of writing (1998) it is up for sale and has potential as a restaurant. It is obviously an old building, probably dating from the 15th century but has been added to and altered. The name Stanks could refer to the marshy nature of its position but there is evidence of farm buildings and it is such a large building that it could possibly have been a tithe barn for the area, which would explain why it has managed to survive the centuries. One end of the building is more ecclesiastical looking, with mullioned windows and some decoration to the window jams. This is thought locally to have been built in the 17th century by a Major Greatheads as his private chapel. The Major was probably involved in a local plot called the Farnley Wood plot to depose Charles 2nd. This unsuccessful plot lead to twenty two schemers being executed.

Leaving the barn go down hill to reach Dewsbury Road. Turn right and go under the railway bridge. You will soon come to the Tommy Wass`s public house. There actually was a real Tommy Wass way back in history but he was a farmer. The old farm house building is probably hidden in the fabric of the present public house. Cross the road here and in order to return to your starting point go along Old Lane. After the industrial buildings on your left a path veers to the left behind the houses and brings you to the car park and to the Church of St Marys.

CITY TO TEMPLE NEWSAM

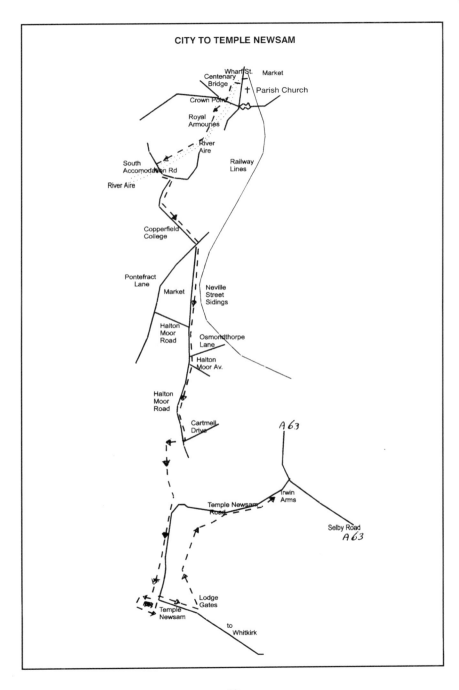

Wharf St.
Centenary
Bridge
Market
Crown Point
† Parish Church
Royal
Armouries
River
Aire
Railway
Lines
South
Accomodation Rd
River Aire
Copperfield
College
Pontefract
Lane
Market
Neville
Street
Sidings
Halton
Moor
Road
Osmondthorpe
Lane
Halton
Moor Av.
Halton
Moor
Road
Cartmell
Drive
A 63
Irwin
Arms
Temple Newsam
Road
Selby Road
A 63
Lodge
Gates
Temple
Newsam
to
Whitkirk

CITY CENTRE TO
TEMPLE NEWSAM

Start: Leeds Civic Trust Heritage &
Design Centre,
Wharf Street, The Calls, Leeds LS2 7EQ   Map: O.S. S/E 23/33 Leeds
Transport: Bus from the Irwin Arms to City Centre 27, 83, 140.
Car Parking: Metered parking at the City Market, across river at Tetleys,
      or at the Irwin Arms and make the bus journey before starting
      the walk.
Description. Mostly surfaced footpaths and bridleways.
Approximately 9km. 5 1/2 miles 2 1/2 hours.

On leaving the Civic Trust Building turn right on Wharf Street, cross High
Court near the sculpture of the World (illuminated at night). Cross to the far
side of The Calls and turn left.

Leeds Civic Trust

The name The Calls fascinates people. No one really knows what the name means but it is certainly one of the oldest streets in Leeds. It could have its origins in the Roman description of a small street, Calley. The street now has a smart hotel and blocks of distinctive waterside dwellings, very central for city living and for visiting business people.

Turn right to cross the River Aire by Centenary Bridge, and turn left to walk along the towpath.

This pedestrian bridge crossing over the river Aire was erected in celebration of the Centenary of Leeds having the status of a City. The bridge takes us over towards Tetleys Brewery Wharf developed by Joshua Tetley & Son as a tourist attraction telling the story of brewing down through the ages. There is also a restaurant, looking over the river, and a shop. This building is in a very different style to many of the old warehouse buildings along the river. It provides a home for Tetleys famous shire horses as well as replica public houses from the past, and some ideas for future drinking and refreshment places.

Walk along the towpath enjoying the vistas of Langtons Wharf across the river (once a builders merchants store).

The Calls

The name Langton reminds us of the previous owner of the site. The Langton brothers were famous for their association with the Isle of Man TT races. The Chandlers next to Langtons is in honour of the corn chandlers who used to supply food for the horses that pulled the boats up the river and worked the Leeds horse tram system.

Royal Armouries

Continue along the towpath and go through the pedestrian way under Crown Point Bridge.

Built in 1840 as a toll bridge, it has recently been widened to take more traffic but the old iron fretted facade was retained. You can see the Weir across the river, the first lock on the Aire and Calder Navigation, and the Royal Armouries building. The Aire and Calder Navigation was an early improvement to the river to enable more goods to be transported by water to the East coast ports and then to the continent.

The Royal Armouries, formidably built in 1996 to exhibit weapons of war and demonstrate important scenes from history. There are tableaus of hunting, shooting, jousting etc. You can easily spend the whole day at the Royal Armouries, where there is something of interest for all the family. Across the river are several old red brick buildings that have recently been renovated.

Walk on past the Armouries and the new student accommodation flats. At the canal side there is a rather delightful mile post with a frog on top, showing that you are now 1 mile from Leeds and 7 miles from Methley. This part of the walk is also a feeder route for the Trans Pennine Trail. When you reach South Accommodation Bridge go under the bridge and ascend the steps on the right up to the road level. Turn right and cross the river. There is a broad footpath across the bridge towards the traffic lights. Turn right on Knowsthorpe Crescent, cross over Knowsthorpe Lane, and continue on the right hand side of Cross Green Lane, passing Copperfield College on your right, to reach Pontefract Lane - sign posted to the Wholesale Market.

Cross Pontefract Lane, turn right for five metres and then fork left on a wide tarmac path, passing through the barrier for cars. Halton Moor Road is a bridle path with street lighting. At the start of this straight path there are allotments on your left, then Neville Hill Railway sidings.

To the right are extensive buildings for the Wholesale Market, and, rather surprisingly, a cricket ground. Continue straight ahead and join the tarmac road near the end of Osmondthorpe Lane and Halton Moor Avenue. The bridle path continues ahead with fields on your right, and brings you to houses and flats at Cartmell Drive. Turn right on the wide sandy surfaced track at the cross roads here. There are some stables on your left. Ascend the rise to reach the Ordnance Survey post after about 150 metres, and turn left through the barrier which prevents motor vehicles entering the drive. The wide gravel track has Halton Moor Wood on the left, and views across Temple Newsam Golf Course ahead and to the right.

Take care walking across the golf course. Join the tarmac road past the sports ground on your left. Then leave the road to walk up the avenue of sycamore trees which will bring you to Temple Newsam House.

Temple Newsam House and the 917 acres estate were purchased by Leeds City Council in 1922. The history of the house goes back to the Domesday Book, and it well worth having a look in the information centre near to the restaurant in the stable block. The house has a wonderful collection of 18th century furniture, particularly of Thomas Chippendale, who was born in Otley. There are many other features and things very much of local and national interest. The Royal connection which brings many visitors, especially those of Scottish descent, is the Darnley room where it is said Lord Darnley was born. Lord Darnley married Mary Queen of Scots, but probably lived to regret this. The grounds of the house are beautiful especially in May/June when the rhododendrons are in bloom. The Home Farm and the rare breed centre are especially loved by children. There is much of interest and several enjoyable hours could be spent here. At the time of writing the house is not open all the time, so check before you leave if you intend to visit the inside. Information can be obtained from Gateway Yorkshire at the railway station in Leeds. Refreshments are available in the cafe in the Stable block.

Retrace your steps to the main carriageway to the house. (This road goes through the grounds and on to Whitkirk and Crossgates. It would be an alternative route back to transport.) Go along the Elm walk which is just to the left of the carriageway (as though going to Whitkirk). At the end there is a small car park and some imposing stone gate posts to your right.

Go through the car park and then turn left on the marked Temple Newsam bridlepath through the woods. Follow the bridle path along the edge of the wood, with the open space to your left. You come to another car park (it may have been a pond or remains of open cast coal mining) take the path to the right here. After 50 metres turn left on another track. Through the trees to the right are some houses. After 150metres you come out of the trees and cross the open ground to Temple Newsam Road . Turn right on Temple Newsam Road and continue along this broad green belt on the right of the road, crossing over the end of New Temple Gate and Plantation Avenue. The road rises slightly here and soon on the right there is a small park with tennis courts and bowling green. Cross yet another road and in about 50 metres you reach the Irwin Arms. (Irwin was the family name of the last owners of Temple Newsam. The coat of arms is on the building). Walk in front of the pub and there is a bus stop to return you to the centre of Leeds.

HORSFORTH, KIRKSTALL AND LEEDS

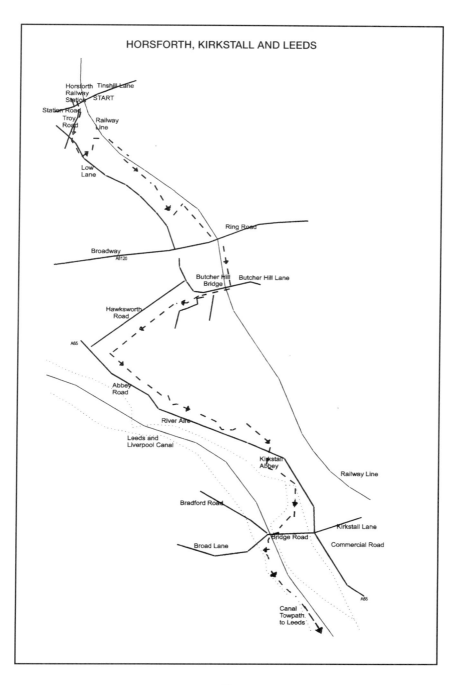

HORSFORTH TO KIRKSTALL AND LEEDS

Start: Horsforth Railway Station.   Map: OS SE 23/33

Transport. By train. 30 minutes service from Leeds.

Bus 63 74A 74B X93.

Car parking: At the Station.

Description: Through woodland footpaths and on the canal towpath.

Approximately 11km. 7 miles 4 hours

The start of this walk from Horsforth gives an opportunity to have a look at this interesting place. Horsforth has a very lively interest in its local history and there is much to be enjoyed and appreciated here. The station is much used by business people travelling to Leeds and Harrogate. The history of the railways in Horsforth itself would be worth exploring. But we are off on our walk back to Leeds.

The Potteries, Horsforth

Leave the station from the north bound platform. To your right you will see what is now a pottery.

> *This building was at one time the Fox and Hounds, a public house on the ground floor and on the upper floor it was a weaving shed. It was bought by the Railway Company to be used by the station master and the ticket office.*

Cross Station Road, taking care, and go along Troy Road. After a slight uphill section pass Low Lane garage and after a further 20metres turn left down the waymarked path.

> *It is worth looking at the buildings as you walk down Troy Road. Many of the new buildings are on sites once occupied by mills. Sadly the old manorial corn mill has now gone, demolished back in the 60s. Brookfoot Mill remains and you can see the hoist still in place from the first storey, the building dates from the 17th century. Brookfoot Mill was when first built called Long Mill, from the family who built the mill, originally as a corn mill. The substantial stone house, now used by the business occupying the old mill buildings, was more than likely built by Richard Long.*

Walk down the lane by the side of the mill and old house passing through a barrier down to a small stream. Cross the fine stone clapper bridge. Keep straight forward into the wood. The cobbled path bends to the right uphill and soon reaches a wall. The path continues alongside this wall. The railway

Horsforth Station

is to the left beyond this wall. Pass two interesting old standing stones (possibly old gateways). Continue on the path, shortly turning left under a railway bridge, then immediately right with the railway on your right. The path soon joins a tarmac path with modern street lighting. Keep right here, and very soon turn right off this path through the wood. Keep on the main path turning right and again go under the railway bridge. Bear left on the broad path which goes down hill, just before a bridge over the stream turn sharply left past a dog kennels, called Tweed House.

Turn right on the path along the edge of a field going down hill towards the Leeds Ring Road. Cross the Ring Road, taking great care, and turn left to go under the large railway bridge. Immediately turn right on the waymarked grassy, uphill, footpath. At the top of the rise on the left can be seen buildings and playing fields belonging to Abbey Grange School. (The name could be a reference to a grange belonging to Kirkstall Abbey.) At the main road turn right down hill passing Lea Farm Road on your left. Soon a small footpath to the left leads into a modern housing development, Cragside Close. Go to the right, follow round a left bend, then take the path to the right entering Hawksworth Woods.

In the past much stone must have been quarried here, and probably used to build many of the houses. It is interesting to see the large blocks of stone lying on the ground.

Continue on through the wood bearing left on the broad path. At the sign posted junction of paths turn left towards Vesper Road, parallel with Abbey Road. In winter a group of buildings connected with Kirkstall Forge on the banks of the river Aire can be seen through the trees.

The famous Kirkstall Forge is probably one of the oldest forges still in existence. It is believed to have been started by the monks at Kirkstall Abbey. If you are fortunate you may hear the sound of the tilt hammer making a dull thud as it produces the desired shapes.

Continue on the path parallel with Abbey Road. You will come to housing at Vesper Road. Make your way through the estate by turning right on Vesper Road, left for a few metres on Woodhall Drive, then right on Abbeydale Mount, left on Abbeydale Way, right on Abbeydale Vale, to reach Vesper Gate Drive. At the junction of Vesper Gate Drive with Abbey Road turn left along Vesper Lane. Pass the large red brick house called Vesper Lodge, to reach a large open area of grassland and a tarmac road which leads to Abbey House Museum car park and childrens play ground.

The museum building was developed from the original gate house of the 12th century abbey. After the Dissolution of the Monasteries in 1539 by Henry 8th, the last Abbot, John Ripley, lived the rest of his life in the gatehouse, which he had converted to a dwelling house. The building was then used by successive important people in Leeds, the Saviles, Brudenelles, Butlers, until Col. John North bought the estate and presented the Abbey and grounds to Leeds Corporation in 1890. In 1925 plans were in place to make it into a museum and it has evolved into the very popular place that it is today. The Museum illustrates the lives of ordinary people and scenes from the ordinary streets in the city of Leeds in previous days.

Across the road from the museum is the towering black building of Kirkstall Abbey itself. You have the choice of a picnic lunch by the childrens' playground, a visit to the museum, or to cross the road (by the pedestrian crossing) to visit the Abbey.

The Cistercian Abbey at Kirkstall was built in a remarkably short time, especially when you consider the few tools available to the builders at that time. It was built in about 30 years from stone brought down the river, probably on flat bottomed boats from the area now known as Bramley falls. The stone used from these quarries

Kirkstall Abbey

is a very resilient stone, especially good for our climate, in that it repels water. This is quite likely the reason that it has existed to our present day. The stone was exported in great quantities all over the world. We are very fortunate to have such a complete collection of monastic buildings so near to the centre of a modern city. It can be argued that the success of the whole area owes much to the industry of the monks. They not only devoted themselves to the power of prayer (the last prayers for the evening - Vespers - are remembered in the names of neighbouring streets) but also kept many thousands of sheep, built and established outlying farms, created works of art, made iron tools etc.

It is known that merchants visited Yorkshire Abbeys from as far away as Italy to buy wool. The grounds of the Abbey, it's Guest House, the rock map of Great Britain and the many surrounding buildings are well worth examining. There is a fine view across the River Aire. The river was of course the main reason for the establishment of the monastery here.

After a look at the Abbey, its cloisters etc., walk to the left with the river on your right. Keeping in the grounds of the Abbey, the path continues on past the weir, waterman's cottage, and mill race. Keep to this path crossing a foot bridge. Turn left with the mill race and a large stone building, originally Abbey Mills, on your left.

This brings you on to Bridge Road, Kirkstall. If you wish you may take a bus back to the centre of Leeds from here. If you decide to continue the walk turn right towards the bridge over the river. Pass the war memorial on the right. Allders store provides an opportunity for refreshments, toilets etc. The magnificent cast iron bridge (1912) over the river provides an opportunity to see the open space where many acres of rhubarb were grown.

There was certainly a bridge over the river in the 17th century as it is recorded that the bridge was broken down during the fighting in the civil war. The Parliamentary forces who had hoped to cross the river by the bridge had to retrace their steps and enter the town via Woodhouse Moor.

Leave the bridge and bear right. Immediately cross the Leeds and Bradford Road at the traffic lights, taking care, and using the central refuge. This is a very busy crossing. Keep to the right, pass Hollybush Farm and steel gates.

Cross Broad Lane at the traffic lights. The path to the canal towpath goes from the corner of Wyther Lane and Broad Lane, passing through stone pillars.

An Act was passed in 1770 for the making of a navigable cut or canal from Leeds Bridge in the county of York to the North Ladys walk in Liverpool in the county Palatine of Lancaster and from thence to the river Mersey. The original survey carried out by John Longbotham planned a canal of 108 miles long. Another survey by the celebrated James Brindley led to the final length of the canal being fixed at 127 miles, at a cost of £1,200,000. The difficulties of completing the canal over the Pennines meant that sections of the canal at Leeds and at Liverpool were completed fairly quickly, but it was to take until 1816 till it was finally finished. Unfortunately it was not many years later that railways were invented and so the canal was superseded.

However the walk back to Leeds along this stretch of the canal (approx 4kms) is very pleasant, combining easy walking, rural surroundings with the opportunity to see waterfowl and other birds as well as passing Armley Industrial Museum and other interesting buildings. The River Aire, the railway and the canal are all very close and you pass underneath several road and railway bridges. The views of Leeds include Leeds General Infirmary, the old Grammar School spire, the dome of the Town Hall and many other important buildings. The towpath passes the site of the old coal wharfs for the old electricity generating plant. The numbers on the bridges register the number out from Liverpool. Passing underneath the Leeds & Bradford railway bridge (railway dating from 1846-7 surveyed by George Stephenson) you can see to the left the amazing length of the river weir for the mills at Armley. A truly awesome sight when the river is in spate.

This site has been used for corn and fulling mills from at least 1559. In 1788 it was probably the largest fulling mill of its day. It was built by Thomas LLoyd, a Leeds merchant. A disastrous fire in 1804 lead to the mill being re built in a more fire proof manner by Benjamin Gott, who also made good use of the river power. A visit to Armley Mills gives a fascinating picture of the development of many of the industries of Leeds including textiles, tanning, printing, photography, steam engines, cinema etc. It is an eye opener to any one new to Leeds to see the diversity of trades that contributed to the development of the city. To visit the museum take the stone steps at the side of the bridge and then go over the bridge to the road down to the museum.

The bridge over the canal was originally made of iron but was replaced in concrete in 1979 though the fine cast iron balustrade has been retained. Keep on the towpath passing under the Leeds & Thirsk railway viaduct. This is a fine piece of railway architecture.

The viaduct was made to the design of Thomas Grainger in 1846 to carry the line across the Aire valley. The part over the canal is very attractive with rusticated niches.

On the right hand side the banking of the canal becomes steeper. It is thought that at some time in the past a castle existed on this site. It certainly would have commanded a wonderful view and with a little imagination you can understand this thought. In the 19th century the site was developed by Samson Fox as the Leeds Forge where iron was originally made. Later in 1883 steel was made here mainly for railway engines and rolling stock. Signs of the buildings can still be seen across the canal. Continuing you come to Spring Garden Lock. This lock lifts or lowers boats for 9ft. On the side of the factory near the lock there is a large mural created by Graeme Wilson, a local artist, showing people at work. You reach Castleton Mill, a four storey red brick mill of 1838 with its great semi circular stair tower projecting out. It was originally built for the flax industry. You pass St. Ann's Lock with a lift of 4'6" then a modern concrete bridge over the canal replacing that built by Benjamin Gott who wished to improve the way to his Bean Ing Mill (now the site of the Yorkshire Post building). The next bridge is the Leeds & Thirsk railway bridge of 1846. On the left hand side of the canal is a crescent shaped repair shop of 1870. It is something of a miracle that these buildings have survived. Monk Bridge comes next, originally dating from 1827 but the present one dates from 1886, constructed by the City Engineer. This bridge is nicely decorated with Leeds coat of arms.

You are nearly back into the centre of Leeds, and at the lock that connects the Leeds Liverpool canal with the river Aire and the Aire and Calder navigation, making a waterway right across the country. Near Granary Wharf is the first bridge on the Leeds Liverpool canal and the building that was originally used by the canal company as a meeting room for the directors (1770). This first bridge is a very fine stone bridge with rusticated decoration. It is worth going over this bridge to get a better view of two imposing towers.

These towers, now preserved, were built by Col. T . W . Harding for his factory where they made pins for wool, flax, cotton, and silk combing. The smaller tower with the octagonal top is a copy of the campanile (bell tower) of the Palazzo del Signore in Verona. It was designed for use as a chimney by Thomas Shaw in 1864. The larger tower was a copy of Giottos campanile of 1334 at the Duomo in Florence. This large tower has decorated bands of coloured brickwork instead of marble as the original had, the mock window openings are filled with glittering panels of golden tiles.

This is the end of the walk and it only remains to walk through Granary Wharf under the magnificent piece of Victorian engineering known as the Dark Arches that are literally under the City Station. When you emerge from the Dark Arches and the view of the rushing waters of the river Aire you are in Neville street. Turn left in to City Square.

The Canal Near Granary Wharf

PUDSEY FULNECK TONG AND COCKERSDALE

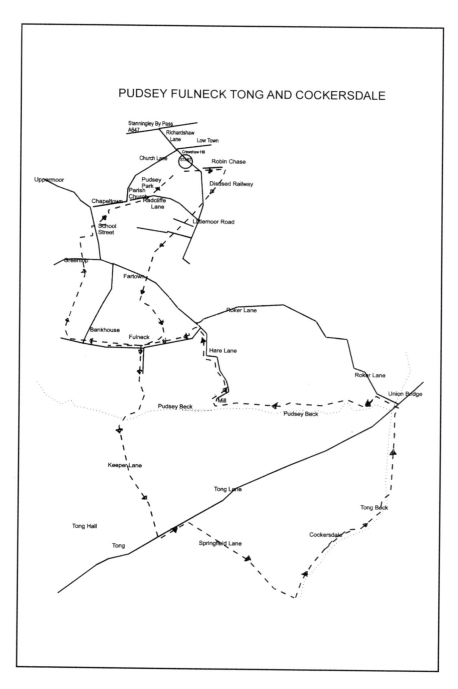

PUDSEY, FULNECK, COCKERSDALE AND TONG

Start: Pudsey Leisure Centre, off Church Lane.   Map: OS SE 23/33
Transport: Bus 4 5 5B 14 40 44 88 90 90A 92 X11 X14
Car Parking: Large car park behind the Leisure Centre.
Description: By road, field, and woodland paths, some small hills.
Approximately 10km. 6 miles 3 hours.

Pudsey is proud of its long history going back at least 800 years, the Domesday Book included a description of the manor of Podechesaie. Later Pudsey developed as an independent township and with the prosperity derived from its thriving woollen, and later boot and shoe manufacturing industries, was granted a Charter of Incorporation in 1899 when it became a Borough with its own Mayor and Corporation.

By 1937 the town had become much larger with the addition of the adjacent villages of Farsley and Calverley. However when there was local government re-organisation in 1974 Pudsey became part of Leeds City. If you have time to take a look at Pudsey either before or after your walk you will soon see that Pudsey retains its character and has some large and interesting buildings as well as the intriguing and welcoming Booths Yard complex.

Go across the front of the Leisure Centre and turn right with the Leisure Centre entrance on your right. Turn right at the T junction down Crawshaw Hill to Robin Lane. Cross Robin Lane, turn right for a few metres, then left down Robin Chase. At the bottom go part of the way along the footpath between houses numbers 29 and 31, and turn right on another narrow gravel path for a few metres to join the path along the track of the disused railway. At the end of the first short section bear right, cross the road and go through a stile to continue on the old railway track for a second short section.

Go through a stile, cross straight over the road again keeping the bridge on your right, to another stile and continue on the old railway track for a third short section.

Go through another stile, cross the tarmac road with the railway bridge on your left to a stile and a path on the old railway track for a fourth short section.

At the end of this fourth section the stile leads in to a tarmac surfaced ginnel. Turn left for a few metres to the road. Turn left, over the railway bridge, and after 50 metres turn right at the finger post and go along the paved footpath passing round a sports ground and housing estate to reach a road by the side of the Regent Inn.

Cross straight over and walk up Hillthorpe Road. At the top turn left along a track passing the gates of Fairmont on your right. Go straight ahead at the cross tracks to reach a street. Turn right for a few metres then left just before Ashdene Close along a broad track which soon follows round to the right and descends in to Fulneck.

We will be returning to Fulneck later so that you can explore, but now we are going to continue on our walk.

Fulneck School

Turn right for 50 metres passing the settlement. Take the first road to the left going down hill, signed to the golf course.

As you turn down the hill notice the wall on the right. The horse shoe shaped area on top of the wall was once the place where carriages used to turn round. There was an inn in Fulneck in 1761 which provided refreshment and rest for travellers. Being so near to the Moravian settlement it was a course of constant worry to the temperate members. So by the 1830s the inn had become a temperance hotel. By 1900 it was a guest house and later became part of the school buildings. Disaster struck in the 1960s when building work was going on. The foundations slipped so the building collapsed to a heap of rubble. Where the building was there is now a space in front of the Fulneck cafe which still provides refreshment for travellers. It is worth going inside for a coffee or meal. Evidently the building was once used as a druggist and general store and the people who run the cafe have managed to retain some of the interesting fitments from that time.

Go down hill past the carriage-turn-round. Take the path to the left down some steps before reaching the Golf Club. You are now on an old paved way. After a steep section the paving ceases. Go straight ahead across the fairway of the golf course (taking care to watch for flying golf balls). The path first heads towards the large tree in the middle of the fairway, then slightly left to join the path alongside Pudsey Beck.

Turn right for about 150metres to a track junction, turn left, cross the footbridge and ascend steeply up Keeper Lane. This can be muddy.
At the top of the bank Keeper Lane is surfaced with tarmac and joins Tong Lane. The remains of the old smithy and pinfold have been preserved at the corner together with an old metal water pump dating from about 1840. Turn right to visit the Church.

Only a short distance up the road to the right passing delightful well preserved village housing, are the Greyhound pub and the Church, re-built in 1727. Outside the Churchyard stand the stocks and a mounting block. If the Church is locked (probable) you may obtain the key from the Church Farm house across the road. Inside there are monuments to the Tempest family who undoubtedly endowed the Church. Just a few metres further will bring you to Tong Hall built by the Tempests in 1702. The house is unusual for this area in that it is built in brick, looking very different from the more common stone. The house is now being used by a commercial firm but it is hoped that they have managed to retain some of its features including carvings by Grinling Gibbons.

Return to the village pump. Pass Keeper Lane on your left and continue along Tong Road. Ignore the footpath signposted off to the right which passes through the farm (H.Goodall & Sons). Take the waymarked bridleway down to the right about 200 metres along Tong Road from the pump and pinfold.

This is Springfield Lane, and it leads down to Cockersdale. Turn left along the good path with Tong Beck on your right for about 1¼kms, then cross over the footbridge (this is the third footbridge you reach, with a black angle iron hand rail) and continue with Tong Beck now on your left along the bottom of Nan Whins Wood to reach Tong Lane at Union Bridge.

Cross Tong Lane and go along Roker Lane for 150 metres passing an old mill on the left. Just before a white house, where the road bends to the right, take the footpath on your left which leads along with Pudsey Beck on the left for about 1¼kms to the far side of an old mill with a tall metal chimney. Turn right across the mill yard and up Hare Lane, steep, to reach the junction with Roker Lane, and the gateway leading in to Fulneck on your left.

Fulneck village is quite unique, little changed over the 250 years since its foundation. There are many interesting buildings to look at as you walk through along the street. A Leeds Civic Trust blue plaque marks the Victorian terrace house on your right where one of Yorkshires cricketing heros was born - Len Hutton or Sir Len Hutton as he became known. He was born on 23rd June 1916 and first played cricket alongside his father with Fulneck School. From there he played with the well respected cricket club of Pudsey St. Lawrence at the age of 12. He was only 13 when he started at Headingley. From then on he had a glittering career scoring many centuries for the County and England.

His test match one innings score of 364 runs was a record for many years.

Continue along the village street, passing the art shop, to come to the school buildings.

The foundation of the Moravian settlement, established in Fulneck since 1744, originated in

House near Tong

78

1457. The movement was encouraged to set up a religious house in Yorkshire through the help given by Rev. B. Ingham and others, and first established a small settlement at Lightcliffe, near Halifax. It was not until 1744 that land at "Fallneck" in Pudsey was purchased by Rev. Ingham on which to build a Chapel originally called "Lambs Hill". In 1763 it became known as Fulneck. A Church was built and later a school for girls and boys. Many famous people have been pupils here including Diana Rigg, the actress, Richard Oastler the child philanthropist, and Herbert Asquith, Prime Minister of England. There is a second plaque on the wall near the Church which commemorates Benjamin H. la Trobe architect of the White House, Washington, born here in 1764. Obviously there is a lot more to learn about the history of Fulneck and if you are in the village on a Wednesday or Saturday in the Spring and Summer months you may visit the museum .

On reaching the end of the village buildings keep ahead, again passing the Fulneck cafe and restaurant on the left, and continue on to the Bank House Inn, ignoring the footpath signed to the right..

Bank House End was once the site of a toll house. This was at the position of many paths including Scholebrook Lane, (known locally as Ass Lane because of the number of pack horses that used to make their way from Tong to Pudsey).

Go straight ahead, across the road and passing the pub car park on the right, pass a house called Hunters Folly on the left, towards Nesbit Hall.

About 50 metres before Nesbit Hall the path leads up the bank to the right, then turns right across the middle of the field to join a narrow track between the fields. At the top end of this narrow track there are good views all round, and one can see the bulk of Pudsey Parish Church which you are aiming to reach.

The walk now leaves the fields and countryside and passes through streets and houses.

At the end of the narrow track pass Hutton House on the right, cross over the road and continue ahead through a ginnel to cross another road and continue ahead in to Smalewell Close. Keep straight ahead on the footpath, turn right in front of houses numbers 25 &23A and the Community Centre to join the main road Greenside. Cross over and turn left for 100metres. Turn right along School Street, passing Pudsey United Reformed Church. Turn left up a ginnel between the Church and Victoria Terrace. Walk past the backs of five houses and turn left to the Golden Lion. Turn right through the picnic area on to the main road, Chapeltown. Turn right, pass the War Memorial on your right, and opposite Pudsey Parish Church, go ahead down Radcliffe Lane. Cross Radcliffe Lane and at the end of the Churchyard go through the gates in to Pudsey Park.

> *Pudsey people can enjoy this Park established by successful industrialists in the 19th century. In the Park are an aviary, conservatory, bowling green, and childrens play ground. It is a delightful spot for young and old.*

Walk through the park to return to the Leisure Centre for public transport back to Leeds and the car park.

Tong Hall